IN ENCHANTMENT OF ETERNITY

Kalu Onwuka

Granada Publishing

Los Angeles, California

In Enchantment of Eternity

Published in Los Angeles, California by Granada Publishers. Granada Publishers is wholly owned by Granada Publishing Company, Los Angeles, California.

Granada Publishing titles may be purchased in bulk for educational, business, fundraising or sales promotional use. For information please e-mail **sales@granadapublishing.com**.

Library of Congress Cataloging-in-Publication data.

In Enchantment of Eternity/Kalu Onwuka

LCCN: 2013957839

ISBN: 978-0-9900203-1-8

ISBN: 0990020312

Printed in the United States

Dedication

I will like to dedicate this book, which is part of *Poems in Faithfulness to the Divine* series, to all those who have shared the gifts of light and love with me either in formal or informal settings. You are too numerous to count but you have my heart-felt gratitude. I will also like to share the series with all those who love poetry and the everlasting beauty of simple words fitly spoken. Oftentimes in life, the will to act is not so much enabled in what is said but how it is said.

Acknowledgments

As always, I will first like to acknowledge Christ Jesus as the Lord of my life. He is my muse and it is his Spirit that enables me to write. Also, I will like to acknowledge that it is not possible to see through an undertaking such as *Poems in Faithfulness to the Divine* series without the loyal support of family, friends and well-wishers. You have all been there from the conception, writing and the publication process. I will like to acknowledge all your help for you continue to give me cause to hope for the best in mankind. It is such goodness that you share that evokes the pure love and good hope for better extolled within these poems.

CONTENTS

CONTENTS

CONTENTS

CONTENTS

CONTENTS

CONTENTS

OTHER BOOKS BY KALU ONWUKA INCLUDE-

(Poetry)

Anthems in the Glorious Dawn

A Splendid Awakening

Tones of the Stellar

The Melody of Light

(Studies for Spirit, Mind and Body)

Nuggets of Resurrection

Pulses of the Divine Heart

Etching for the Faithful Heart

No Hurry to Horeb

(Quotations and Insights)

Capsules of Divine Capsule

All titles are available as paperbacks or e-books and may be purchased through many retail outlets and distribution channels. All titles may also be purchased through Granada Publishers at **granadapublishing.com.** The author can be contacted through his website at **kaluonwuka.com.**

FOREWORD

This book of poetry titled *In Enchantment of Eternity* is the second volume in the *Poems in Faithfulness to the Divine* series. It is a compilation of original poems that speak about spiritual transformation and places that man must leave behind in order to find the better in life.

There are ninety four original poems in this volume that are woven from different strands into a common thread of pure love and good hope. The poems strike a distinctive tune that resonates in the heart. There are such poems that speak about whispers of divine love, the best that is found when mind is focused above, the compassionate heartbeat of the divine, the true value that lies within man, the new vision availed to the reconfigured soul, the brilliant eloquence of pure light, and victory that finds the ready.

The book makes for an interesting reading in ways that the perceptive reader will find to be enriching and spiritually nourishing. It is a must-have for anyone of faith who loves poetry as well as others with lingering questions about faith.

Kalu Onwuka

For Circumcised Hearts

Heed the man within pleads a voice
Inaudible yet quite clear as crystal
Language sought after since Babel
That speaks deep from man's heart

Dare to look within it pleads with all
Let no darkness be found therein
Save truth and light locked tightly
In the sweet embrace called love

Language of heaven that says it all
Is for circumcised hearts to know
Such that the deaf can hear clearly
In warmth that the blind can feel

Tis called sweet language of love

Let its healing essence flow freely

So that men's hearts can be tuned

To hear Life's soothing melodies

End

Man for All Seasons

The faithful that has the divine anointing
Also has pre-ordained appointments to keep
Destiny calls him to be Creation's guardian
Charges him to help goodness abound below

Man that understands the purpose of life
Calls every living thing by appropriate name
Just like Adam before his fall from grace
Knew the purpose for the plants and animals

A mind that is in harmony with the divine
Same the faithful believer can have in time
Purpose and order will define things for him
To be a good caretaker in Creation's garden

The curator of things pronounced to be good
By no less an authority than the divine Father
Thru Summer, Winter, Fall and Spring times
Is a man for all seasons there when it counts

End

Pieces of God's Heart

God's kingdom on earth is a divine mansion
Some faithful souls in that abode do dwell
Such glimpse the pattern of the heavenly
And strive to replicate same on earth below

Those are the tabernacles fit to be enlarged
Noble sons who live to do as the Father bids
Thru their endeavors and collective efforts
Heaven on earth is being availed to humanity

God's heart is the mansion grand and lovely
The sons are rooms in many hues and colors
Pieces of his heart remade in love by his will
As only way for man to know true fulfillment

Pieces of God's Heart (Cont'd)

Pieces of the father's heart are in every land

Stars that shine brightly under earth's dark veil

The darker the place and more wicked the lot

Therein is the light of the son more blazing

End

A Living Network

Men in communion with the Father
Are extensions of the divine on earth
And conduits for those things which flow
From Heaven's throne to earth below

Such souls are like personal computers
Joined with the super-computer Father
To all connected in this network of love
Knowledge is availed for victory in life

Takes the power from the Holy Spirit
To enable the computers in the network
Content and information shared therein
Is availed to the user by the Holy Ghost

A Living Network (Cont'd)

A beehive of information this network is
With wisdom of the divine coursing thru
In an ever flowing stream that is pure
From the starry to darkly places in light

Truth assures the integrity of the system
And keeps the enclave humming in faith
Tis like a firewall that shields the network
And separates things that are out of tune

The components plugged in the network
Are certified in truth to be of good works
For truth is the transformer that makes
Divine power to work mightily for man

End

Nymphs of Faith

The standard bearers for the people
Are called to lead the blind in the way
Such receive the key of understanding
To guide their steps in life's endeavors

Divine mercies are ordered for them
As men who live for cause of goodness
So things conceived in heaven above
Can come to be duly realized on earth

Tis an assembly of the merciful in love
Not for those who love not the truth
But part of an ordained universal web
That embodies the spirit of new dawn

Nymphs of Faith (Cont'd)

Such are the seedlings for the new age

Best of humankind kept to save itself

As nymphs groomed in cocoon of love

Under the attentive care of Providence

End

The Third Eye

The man that has the gift of perception
Is equipped with a third eye that most lack
He's given to see through the darkly veil
From the perch that is higher and purer

From the starry abode man looks ahead
To the new place of renewal and hope
For backwards leads to a misguided past
To the accusatory and the recriminatory

Man bestowed with the true gift of sight
Is rejected by most save the faithful few
He's a seer not understood by the blind
And need not defend himself before such

The Third Eye (Cont'd)

The future vindicates and validates in time

To bring the fulfilling in life to the 'seer'

In reward for keeping company with Truth

And for the faithful stewardship of wisdom

End

Fulfillment in Godliness

The entry way is a channel of light
That leads man to Love and into Life
For him to seek by any other means
Is to harvest in the field of bitterness

Disappointments do attend the way
When man trusts not to live by faith
Material goods is best he can gain
But to his surprise that won't suffice

Hunger he craves in the place within
The inner longing that haunts him so
Deep within the depths of his soul
Can be satisfied when spirit awakes

Fulfillment in Godliness (Cont'd)

To seek fulfillment and consolation
Through possessions and acquisitions
Quite a quick way to bankrupt the soul
And be left with fool's gold at best

Tis the guiding light of the North Star
That leads to certainty and fulfillment
Only emptiness and wantonness is left
When man wanders from truth's laws

End

Rain Man

Takes wings of the eagle to mount up
And be bestowed with a grander vision
In light that comes from meat of truth
To crown the faithful with divine wisdom

To see clear pictures within life's scripts
From the perch of the exalted heights
Is to stumble no more under the veiled
But to know in fullness in all that matters

The earthy spirits dwell in lowly places
And lack the wings that lift up the spirit
Such that cannot soar to receive the pure
Are left to traverse beaten tracks below

Rain Man (Cont'd)

The low clouds of the sweet and easy
Are vapors of hot air that bear no rain
And fade away under scrutiny of light
To be dispersed by the winds of the times

The rain clouds are only found up high
In a starry realm where the eagles soar
Tis pure water that sustains true living
So life and goodness may abound in full

Up in the mountain pervaded with life
For only the pure of heart to ascend
There the cleansed in truth are baptized
With the essence of life's everlasting

Rain Man (Cont'd)

The baptized is called by the divine Spirit

To be a rain man who bears living water

As destiny demands and love urges him

Within Life's unending dance of eternity

End

Victory's Dome

For ascension to the starry heights
Much has to be willingly sacrificed
To stand on top of the Holy Mount
Asks for a full commitment thru love

The mystic dew of divine anointing
Is by conversation in heavenly places
Reassuring rod and comforting staff
Are afforded after the token is paid

Gone are yesterdays to be no more
When man is reborn in light thru faith
For a future dawns and beckons him
With much promise and good hope

Victory's Dome (Cont'd)

The misdeeds of the past are forgiven
As such provided lessons well-learned
The corruptible and worldly gone too
From him who has found hope at last

New man of veiled and sacred truths
Lives to guide all who are empty within
Has no time to waste or effort to spare
When many are blind and need to see

End

Immunized in Goodness

The man in covenant with the divine
Travels in light to the heavenly places
He's an elect thru whom grace flows
In goodness and mercy to the lacking

Man that lives to bear up the infirm
With no thanks or praise from many
But doubt and derision from most
Knows that time will honor his deeds

Humiliation and rejection will come
Also hurts and scorn many to count
But the innocent is well-protected
For Benevolence is there to attend

Immunized in Goodness (Cont'd)

Man that performs in noble service

Gets to live in immunity of godliness

For the past has been made powerless

And impotent to touch destiny's own

End

Rehabilitating Eden

The man on life's great journey
Does walk as a god among men
To perform the two-step dance
In love between heaven and earth

Tis the rain dance to summon life
In good that's perfect from above
To refresh the famished on earth
Such souls that yearn for new life

The worthy sacrifices made in love
Are offerings well received by God
So a man's petitions and requests
Can be granted thru his prayers

Rehabilitating Eden (Cont'd)

The true and diligent labor in light
For rehabilitation of Eden's glory
From humanity's westerly sunset
To new awakenings from the east

Tis hand of wisdom there to guide
So man can have a new take on life
As he erases the mistake of Adam
To lift the curse of his yesterdays

End

Forward to Glory

The man within emerges to lead forward
To sever the ties of the misguided past
Days gone by that attempt to hold back
From promises and glory of the future

Pain and hurt often do linger as ghosts
From broken dreams and false promises
From disappointments and deep wounds
At hands of ravenous and capricious men

Such pains are nail marks buried within
That can only be soothed and healed
By the balm of the anointing that oozes
From the caressing hands of the divine

Forward to Glory (Cont'd)

Appointments with Providence to keep

And rendezvous with the Divine to make

All's realized in future safe from the past

Where Light's spawn can have all things

End

At Home Above

Eagle that walks wobbly on earth
Is at home in the exalted heights
Where majesty is very becoming
And nothing is hidden from view

The faithful must banish the fear
From past that cannot touch him
For mind set on the things above
Is given to overcome the world

Where there's no room for fear
Love, life and goodness abound
Keys to good and perfect in life
Await all who dare there to ascend

At Home Above (Cont'd)

There the noble spirits are found

Worthy custodians of the precious

Hearts that beat together in love

As one for the regeneration of life

End

Containers for the New Wine

The tree of life joins heaven and earth
In offerings of hope that never cease
With grace on the lower branches and
Tender mercies on uppermost boughs

Man of faith nourished thru his fears
With the clusters of grace in his youth
Finds tender grapes for the new wine
As he reaches up higher and farther

The content of the new wine is mercy
But only for the souls reborn in light
For such are the custodians of the pure
Able to hold the elixir of the 'gods'

Faithful living in the kingdom of God

Avails taste of divine glory here and now

Demands a short leash on man's flesh

So he can reach for the utmost glory

End

Invitation to Safety

Father reveals so much in these times
To the hearts and souls matured in faith
New visions to see thru darkened veils
In season for man to come 'to full light

Stars of heaven have filled up the night
As the divine hand unfolds the banner
In a great unveiling of the sacred roll
For the honorable and readied in spirit

The stars of heaven are purified souls
Given knowledge of the hidden truths
With third eye of insight to understand
The divine will for the benefit of man

Invitation to Safety (Cont'd)

Sons of light in places over the world

Do foretell and plead with all in love

So that the attentive and the willing

Can join them in safety of God's Ark

End

Hearts Ablaze

The hearts ablaze that glow in truth
Are flames lighted with love of God
As torches that need not make noise
In brilliance that speaks loud enough

The flames of love highlight the way
In ascents and descents up the ladder
As twinkling lights in labors of love
To and fro 'tween heaven and earth

He that desires to see must know
First he has to seek out the true light
For closer and nearer one gets to it
Clearer and better the vision unfolds

Knowledge that is borne from below
Is only for the blind not yet reborn
Tis tinkling cymbal that is much noise
Leads and confines man into a coffin

The way of the world or that of Life
Man can know the right way to go
And can choose wisely through Love
When guided by the light of truth

End

Tamed and Housebroken

The sons of light are soaked in misty dew
Borne of wisdom distilled from ages past
With knowledge of the things yet to come
To point out the way to humanity's future

Such are the timeless spirits that travel
Back and forth through the veil of time
Who are borne on faith's tireless wings
To places far away and beyond the flesh

Much is conveyed thru the sons of light
As pure truth that cleanses men's souls
Such is availed to make the base pure
Even with the most depraved of souls

Tamed and Housebroken (Cont'd)

Truth that changes the foulest to pristine
Also tames the wild soul to be housebroken
So that men can be led into eternity's arms
To be sown into an immortal glorious quilt

The veiled truths are sacred and eternal
Availed only in light and bestowed in love
Such wealth is for the adopted to treasure
In accordance with the order of the divine

End

Charity and Mercy

The true essence of godliness
Is endurance that lasts till end
In hope matured through faith
And mercy that hopes for best

Charity and mercy are twins
Which are hard to tell apart
They avail to man the ability
To speak to all hearts in truth

Mercy makes no room in man
For bitterness to dwell in him
Takes womb of charity to bear
Good fruits in fullness of time

Charity and Mercy (Cont'd)

Both are expedient and ideal

To bring man close to the divine

Good companions they prove

For one on life's grand mission

End

The Light of Charity

Charity speaks a universal language
As the currency of the noble in spirit
Quite a vehicle for man to take along
In his long winding journey thru life

The light of Charity shines lovingly
By pure sacrifices in grace and mercy
To brighten all hearts that it reaches
As mortals learn to take divine steps

Charity is the rare perfected in love
Never for man to contrive or feign
Tis selflessness that embodies things
That shine before heaven and earth

The Light of Charity (Cont'd)

Charity need not parade to be noticed

Seeks not attention and recognition

But it is light that cannot be obscured

For the universe always seeks such out

End

The Way of Light

The way of the divine is purer and higher
Disconnected from man's earthly ways
Realm where the shadowy becomes real
And darkness holds no stakes or claims

No more stumbles under cloudy veils
Or labors in the earthiness of the flesh
But uplifting endeavors in spirit of life
When man walks in light of the higher

When dirt of the false is washed away
Then is the field of dreams come to life
So man can separate the true from false
And no longer see darkly through a lens

The Way of Light (Cont'd)

The misguided teachings of the past
Are the rudimentary much watered down
Needed by the child but not the man
Has to be discarded for real to emerge

The wrappings of the old and dormant
Is peeled off so the new can bask in light
Tis former freed from bondage of death
So that the enduring can come to Life

End

Veil of Tradition

Many do know in part but not in full
Men of concision but not of circumcision
Compassion is for such who are ignorant
And trudge on under life's rudimentary

The misguided assumptions from the past
By tradition's ways that feed not spirit
Do becloud the vision with cold embers
To misplace minds and make men blind

Many are led in judgments by opinions
Of wrong men dead and long deceased
Better for man to use his time on earth
To know the real so he can see the new

Veil of Tradition (Cont'd)

Traditions of the past constitute a veil
That needs to be torn so man can see
A membrane to be punctured in due time
So the new man of light can see the day

The divine Father always does the new
As he teaches man his righteous ways
He opens new doors for seekers to know
More about divine ways and love's gifts

The divine distills the new from the old
And does away with all the irrelevant
Severs and discards what has atrophied
For such is of the dregs of the Pharisees

End

The Right Tool

Falsely accused and wrongly judged
God's chosen and anointed is hated
Not for breaking the new grounds
But for rejecting the tools of the past

But such are tools long worn-out
Ill-suited to break the new grounds
Unknown places beyond the horizon
That can be ploughed only by spirit

The flesh-centric tools of man's past
Are replaced by the new of the spirit
In man reborn in image of the father
To realize the seemingly impossible

The Right Tool (Cont'd)

A special mission for the faithful tools
Entrusted with much by the Father
Models for golden rule that demands
That men speak truth and walk in light

Such are judges of man's inner worth
With no in-equity to be found in them
Given to treat all men as kindred folk
With truth and love as the tool of light

The righteous before heaven and earth
Though misunderstood by many in life
Do labor as sons to bring divine light
To the blind who are willfully ignorant

The Right Tool (Cont'd)

Sons of light are called to chase away

Wickedness that governs men's heart

Borne from hate and denial of truth

With powerful tools of truth and love

End

The Irrepressible

Man comes into knowledge of all-wisdom
So that he can be God's light for the blind
To live with kindness for the benefit of all
As he shares gifts entrusted to him with love

The sinful man can be forgiven and justified
To become a traveler amid unseen helpers
As one worthy among the noble in spirit
Ordained to serve the Father's will on earth

Giants in spirit deemed as gods among men
The highest and worthiest of causes it is
For man prepared to bear all things in love
Whose spirit's given to overcome the world

The man that defies gravity is irrepressible

Has mastered how to soar above all in spirit

And risen from the grave to be raved about

As new that is brave and craves not the old

End

A Way Home

Spiritual flight is man's dream come true
Completion of the journey begun long ago
From the salty marshes to the grassy plains
And finally home to a place in the heavens

A journey that ends in triumphant escape
To the better long desired and hoped for
Source of the living water that sustains Life
That only a chosen few do manage to find

Found by those souls who are led in spirit
And guided by the hand of divine wisdom
Tis the precious found on road less travelled
Not on the broad way preferred by most

A Way Home (Cont'd)

Search for living water is mimicked in nature
By migratory herds that traverse the land
Creatures of unpurified souls that engage
In a fruitless and misguided search on earth

The way to the source of life points upwards
Tis not found thru bravado, might or strength
But found by the humble and lowly in the way
Through sincerity, charity, peace and love

The faithful man deemed lowly by the world
Same is the one exalted by the divine Father
And shown the way to come home into Life
To know himself at last and be known by all

End

Search for the Better

Man's true home is his heavenly future
Not in the irredeemable earthly past
The unpurified soul searches in the past
But the purified looks far into the future

Heavenly home is the continuing city
The enduring that will never pass away
For all who desire and search for better
Up in heaven is where the search ends

To search in the world is to be a victim
As the blind to never know true victory
Who exhausts his limited time on earth
In a search that never reveals the door

Search for the Better (Cont'd)

The blind wonder what life is all about

Man can only know if he comes into Life

Some thru wisdom have come to know

Masters in light who have found the key

End

The Bridge

A great gulf does separate
The creature and his Maker
Some know it is one too far
For man to cross by himself
Save by destiny's timely call

A giant spiritual leap it takes
Not for man's flesh to make
An unseen hand must help
For destiny to avail a bridge
That gets from here to there

The Bridge (Cont'd)

From death to life is a bridge
Thru the helping hand of love
Best to plead and hope for it
It comes in answer to prayers
For man that seeks thru faith

Help by one firmly anchored
On solid rock that moves not
Hope borne of the heavenly
To reach all who cast about
In bid to cross destiny's gulf

End

Hope's Beacon

Sons borne of righteousness
Are anointed in a greater light
As the messengers and proxies
To afford mankind timely help
Needed to span hope's divide

Righteousness calls each man
As mark of good citizenship
In the kingdom of love and life
To walk in light and act in faith
So hope's beacon never dims

Hope's Beacon (Cont'd)

The faithful heart labors in love
With no regard for cost or pain
Keeps hope alive in all he does
So heaven's light can shine forth
And man's hope is ever fulfilled

Laurels, garlands and tributes
In accolades of adoring crowds
Such that acclaim men's deeds
Counts for very little at the end
If LIFE is missing from the list

End

Benefits of Grace

By words and hymns of grace
In thrills and gifts of the spirit
The new in way of faith exults
Enthused with desire and hope

Much rejoicing for the spawn
As he reaps the benefits of grace
That covers and avails him much
In spiritual and material needs

Grace does serve all very well
Tis the protection for the child
Until he can become the man
Strong to stand in faith's battles

Benefits of Grace (Cont'd)

Grace is the gift and the life too
Quite an aggregate of services
To sustain the young in the way
Who is weak and not yet strong

Tis the grand umbrella ordained
As provisional arm of the divine
To cater to the ignorant days
And the transgressions of youth

But there's selfish abuse of grace
That strands many in the way
To be left neither here nor there
Is a sad way to end faith's walk

End

Works that Shine

The works of silver impose not
Never weighty nor yet massive
Shakes off earth's dust to shine
And win God's approving smile

Borne of innocence and hope
By the golden and noble hearts
Works of love that sing in light
In tunes of unmistakable purity

Tis enduring works that sing for all
In heraldic songs of subtle notes
Shines brilliantly for men to see
Shielded from corrosion's decay

Works of the pure twinkle in hope

To evoke sparkles of divine wisdom

Enough to guide all true seekers

Safely through earth's dark passage

End

The Projector

The faithful who aspires for heaven's delights
Must have a to-do list written in his heart
For therein is where the divine Spirit searches
To choose the projects that merit blessing

A foretaste of regeneration is the blessing
As things become less taxing and expedient
So days of struggles, shortfalls and pratfalls
Are soon gone to be forgotten for good

The past with its salty tears of tribulation
Have accomplished its much desired goal
When man has been grafted into the divine
To do the marvelous in power of the spirit

The vehicle of the past often disappointed
Broke down and stranded man on the way
Mired him in clay of disappointment valley
Never could take him to top of victory hill

Man grafted to the divine is never stranded
For he's a utility vehicle good for all seasons
That's powered by sunshine of divine love
And retooled to be fit for all terrains of life

Such is the diligent gardener who will tend
The fruitful trees planted in his earthly lot
As a bee readied for the propagation of life
With honey to produce and glory to savor

End

As Time Stands Still

The love and power of the divine Father
Is harnessed by means of humble prayer
As the sunshine that bathes man in mercy
To help him blend honey's golden potion

The fruits of the orchard are harvested
In the twinkling of an eye it so seems
As time has the illusion of standing still
For one whose prayers are readily heard

He that asks not receives not the precious
For divine helpers wait to serve his cause
A great host near to lend him assistance
To help the faithful do much in little time

Building blocks are there in regeneration
As provisions pre-positioned in the way
There to help all those who trusted in hope
As they ran the marathon that ends in Life

Regeneration remakes the old into the new
For him that has received Life's precious gift
It avails him fulfillment in all that matters
And grants him parking rights in mercy-land

End

Fullness for the Sons

The father knows the estate of all
More so his anointed among men
He affords such a new way of life
In his power and might displayed

Fullness is there for God's chosen
In boundless and limitless gifts
For man that is reborn in light
Can have all the good in creation

The burial bandages of the old
Are wrappings peeled over time
So also the gifts ordained for man
As true riches unveiled only as due

Fullness for the Sons (Cont'd)

Such works that shine before men

Also the glorious that amaze in life

Are wrought through wisdom's craft

And realized in Love's timely order

End

The Unfettered Spirit

Traveler who is on the great journey
Must continue to watch and pray
So that he can remain pure in heart
To serve the divine will in true Light

His spirit is a vehicle to be well kept
Able to go as needed in timely instant
To places within reach and beyond
Ready to serve as goodness demands

The spirit purified in the light of truth
Is concerned with the free and living
Not with the dead and encumbering
That fetters and ties man to a leash

The Unfettered Spirit (Cont'd)

The spirit bound is grounded in service

Lacks in utility, versatility or universality

Has become a pawn and tool of darkness

One no longer good for honorable duty

End

The Strange and Peculiar

The strange and peculiar son of Light
Not easily categorized by his fellows
Lives for God as the Father lives in him
As a man of love who walks in peace

He belongs not with men completely
Yet he belongs with all men in spirit
One seen as incomplete in the world
Is the man that lacks not in any area

He's one blended from different parts
With nectar borne of divine's sunshine
As the imperfect made perfect in love
To be the seminal seed of a new age

A garden of fruitful trees there from

Pleasing for the Father to take a stroll

In communion of mind, body and spirit

For man whose heart is given to God

End

Ode to the Samaritan

Tis the Samaritan who gets the truth
And ends up on the righteous path
Offers up thanks when others do not
And can perceive that which is true

Tis the Samaritan that is intimated
With the wisdom that God is a Spirit
To worship and be known in truth
In communion anywhere and time

Tis the Samaritan that is intimated
With the truth that God doesn't care
For ancestry, pedigree or cathedrals
But seeks after the hearts of men

Ode to the Samaritan (Cont'd)

Tis the Samaritan that does labor on
In the last days and in true charity
To share a true vision of the divine
And bring in the last harvests of souls

Tis the Samaritan who shows all men
That God lives in the heart that bleeds
When faith's robbed and left for dead
And stepped over by an uncaring world

The Samaritan that's little in the world
Is the one that finds intimacy with God
Tis he that becomes life's true treasure
A heart where God makes his home

End

Purified Heart Sees

Only the pure of heart can 'see' God
Not in the flesh as men see others
For he can only be known in spirit
By true fellowship and compassion

He's known by the works of his hand
In nature's feats of creative wonder
And known in the still voice of hope
That speaks to man's heart in peace

Tis God's Spirit that reassures in trials
Through the cries and petitions heard
In timely and kindly responses in love
That says take heart for all will be well

Purified Heart Sees (Cont'd)

For man to know and to 'see' God

He must keep the flesh on short leash

For it is same that chokes the spirit

To hinder and blind the eye within

End

Heart without Guile

Tis the heart that's purified in truth
And not man's flesh the Father seeks
For flesh serves not in the eternal ride
Only good for the brief stay on earth

The purified heart is one without guile
That wills and strives to be obedient
With a true desire to please the Father
So Fortune's face can remain smiling

Contents of faithful hearts are filled
Ever with due and timely knowledge
Such by divine's command experience
Fulfilling riches that love avails in life

The hearts purified in truth do become

Golden censers lit with a flame of love

The divine justifies the actions of such

Who are altars to offer up earth's best

End

Iniquity in the Heart

The ugly heart engages in self-serving endeavors
Aimed to earn the accolades and praise of men
Such is the iniquity often praised by the blind
For it looks good on the outside but is evil within

Man's perfected appearance is used to mislead
By the deceitful purveyors of the fake and false
For the blind are not able to perceive or to know
The contents and evil intentions borne of iniquity

God's anointing imparted through divine grace
Isn't for hearts of iniquity full of guile and deceit
Nor for the impure filled with wicked thoughts
But for the worthy offspring of truth and love

Iniquity in the Heart (Cont'd)

Iniquity refuses to use the same standard for all
And so invites darkness to thrive among mankind
That which discriminates and selects does spawn
Evil that engenders sacrifice of truth and love

Iniquity and wickedness make no room for love
And have no place or welcome for things divine
Will disregard conscience to take un-due gain
As ugly tools used when man is a stranger to God

The seeds buried deep within man do define him
To show up in his work and the fruits of his labor
The worthy and chosen produce the good fruits
But iniquity's offspring are often thorns and briers

End

Beauty for the Chosen

The possessor of the heart chosen by God
Has certain peace that only few ever know
He is the man with his spirit focused above
Who lives in the contentment of godliness

He is given to walk on the high road of life
On path of the true and noble guided in light
Where the meek and gentle are to be found
Who live in quietness borne of good purpose

It is life that seeks not a stage or platform
But lived effacingly in a voluntary humility
With spirit within man ascendant and firm
To always have full sway in all areas of life

The sacrifices made away from the lime light
Of the adulation and the adoration of crowds
Tis work done and life lived for divine glory
So that the beauty of the lily can adorn man

End

Stars of Heaven

The hearts that truly love and fear God
Dwell in spirit amid the lofty and starry
As men transformed into sons of Light
To be the twinkling stars for all to watch

These stars of heaven are the gardeners
Who plant seeds of love to transform men
Although they labor in relative obscurity
Yet they reap in blessed joy of full light

Such pass over unscathed and unharmed
From the wiles and traps of the enemy
Through the miry clay and the minefields
Under God's protection thru life's trials

The Stars of Heaven (Cont'd)

Man is safe from world's evil and darkness

When he's transformed 'to a star of heaven

For God's love is manifested in light's stream

To afford him ultimate protection in mercy

End

Ride the wind

The Spirit is that uplifting divine wind
Knows when to rise and the way to go
Takes God's mind to initiate its course
Govern and justify all its actions too

Just like the electrical current at work
Powers and flows thru a chosen tool
The faithful is that piece of equipment
Re-conditioned for use by the Divine

Takes the flow and power of the Spirit
Thru man to accomplish good works
He that yields in faith is often lifted
To do the lovely that is of good report

Ride the Wind (Cont'd)

Such must hold out his wings of faith
And glide along in glorious liberty
In obedient trust as the spirit leads
So divine's power can be displayed

Tis wind that rises only with occasion
When a certain task needs to be done
Same calls the faithful to ride and soar
Until the task begun is well and done

End

The Ill-Suited Companion

God's chosen is given an earthly helper
A companion divinely ordained for him
He takes the lead and initiative in life
With his helper at dutiful command

There's a mission and purpose that calls
But the helper seems ill-suited for them
With obvious faults and imperfections
When seen with the eyes of the flesh

But God searches with eyes of the spirit
Uses base things to confound the wise
Makes his wisdom and power available
To change the ill-suited into best-suited

The Ill-Suited Companion (Cont'd)

The imperfect with mismatched parts
Is good companion for the faithful man
With short comings come hidden assets
That'll suffice him regardless of defects

The father foresees and figures all out
Always for the best interests of his own
He reveals vital attributes not too soon
Offers them up in due season as needed

God's favorite tool is the faithful man
The helper is a cover from the elements
To shelter him from the irritating bugs
So he can be focused on task at hand

The Ill-Suited Companion (Cont'd)

Faithful help and companion in spirit
Has no complaints but wisdom to seek
'bout ways to bring out the best from all
That love avails man in the light of truth

The horse appointed for God's anointed
To assist in the labors ordained for him
Needless to look at its mouth for it'll do
For its strength lies within not without

End

Patient Love

There is that anointed to secure the future
That takes the seedling 'to reality of harvest
Tis an emblem that speaks 'bout patient love
So hope's promises can be realized as should

Helps to rein in the flesh and tarry in faith
So the ear of the spirit is tuned to the divine
For it takes meditation on the word of truth
To realize all that has been promised in love

The faithful must seek guidance and direction
About all issues amid the challenges of life
He that's given to contemplate and meditate
Will receive all that patient love avails man

End

The Well Digger

The faithful that is borne from love's womb
Is a water bearer for all times and seasons
To nourish and nurse that availed thru faith
In labors of love to secure man's future

He's a well-digger who opens up a fountain
Who knows where to dig when others don't
He makes the call that wakes the dormant
And brings up the water so life can abound

He who digs the well must have a helper
A companion for life to help him in the way
A mate with the gift to draw out the water
And put the waterman's labors to good use

The Well-Digger (Cont'd)

The companion ties it all together for him
So that his labors will not be for naught
Knows to give living water to thirsty souls
On life's errands serving the Master's will

End

In Quietness

The life of meditative and blessed quietness
Seeks for time to be alone with the divine
For pestering and distractive noises do drown
The still small voice that guides man thru life

The noise of the world to him is disquieting
For the solitary traveler on the road of Life
Who travels not in the company of men
But in the company of divine messengers

He does and bears much in blessed quietness
As led by an innate and intimate divine urge
With Providence always at hand to bless
To meet his needs and help him win battles

Such is a host to good things buried within

That are duly revealed in the fullness of time

He's given to recover the forgotten and lost

As one that brings new things into full view

End

Truth

The father of Truth and Love

Can only be known by those

Who speak the same in love

As tis the element that bonds

Faithful man with the divine

He's one after God's heart

The man who lives by truth

And abides by the golden rule

The anointing will be for him

For he lives by a greater law

Truth (Cont'd)

Tis a strait and narrow way
Paved with tablets of truth
The path of righteousness is!
Father's expects all his own
To walk and dwell in its light

Tis language of the faithful
Who live in glorious liberty
Takes truth to set man free
To soar just like the eagle
Up close to God's own heart

Truth (Cont'd)

Truth does afford mankind
Rare peeks behind the veil
Not much have to be said
Only few words are needed
When tongue speaks in kind

Choice tween life and death
All is in power of the tongue
Truth always speaks in grace
And gives God the due glory
So life comes to fully abound

End

Arrow that Lifts

To abide by truth always is to live above the world
With the golden arrow that never misses its mark
For truth registers a distinctive note in man's spirit
And leaves a definitive imprint on the hearts of all

Truth does not seek to impress or to be liked
Only to remove the clutter for the core to shine
Tis food to nourish and sustain the starving soul
So spirit within can rise to soar above the world

Truth uplifts the spirit to places above and beyond
Frees from earthly shackles and from death's box
To defy time and space to get close to the divine
Is the sweet liberty of the starry realm thru light

Arrow that Lifts (Cont'd)

For all who choose not to honor and speak in truth

A sad day when the crown of eternal life is denied

To the unworthy who've used life's gift for naught

Fallen stars trapped in the earthy for denying truth

End

Spiritual Hypocrisy

Man must take care not to mock God
For it is not possible to deceive Him
But faithless man heeds not this truth
On account of his spiritual blindness

Man mocks his Creator all the time
Disparages truth and flaunts the laws
In many ways both told and untold
Some obvious and others concealed

Spiritual hypocrisy is no less spiteful
Most men know and do much talking
About what God desires and requires
But sadly will not live as they profess

Spiritual Hypocrisy (Cont'd)

Religion thrives and faith's trumpeted
But spiritual famine besets the land
As evil and wickedness roam all over
And reign supreme over men's hearts

The young are much discouraged in all
By hypocrisy and prevalent injustice
Sad travesty that breaks faithful hearts
Breaks the Father's heart even more

The hand of Hope is much wearied
From staying the wheel of damnation
Only shameful regret awaits mankind
When judgment hands down a verdict

End

Sow in Spirit

Persistent and consummate desire of man
Is to sow in his flesh and not in his spirit
He's one enamored with earthly materials
Not able to see that flesh profits nothing

To sow in the flesh is to reap corruption
But he that sows in the spirit reaps Life
For material lust keeps man in bondage
To wallow in the miry clay of earthiness

The soul in bondage is deprived of Life
For spiritual death attends him from below
But he that is free is lifted up to receive
Gift of eternal life that alights from above

The heavenly Father is the source of all
Avails man the fulfilling and enduring gifts
His earthly journey becomes meaningless
If creature fails to reconnect with Creator

All that the faithful man goes thru in his life
Is on the path divinely ordained for him
Helps to transform him in a divine image
In steps that lead on to resurrection's day

Tis the process of initiation into eternal life
And into the all-knowing wisdom of God
So that man can walk as a god among men
And speak from place of certain knowledge

End

Weeds of Life

Takes a lot of pruning to untangle a man
From all the un-necessary weeds of life
Also patience and wisdom of love it takes
To wean him from the worldly in little steps

Ugly weeds do clutter the mind's garden
And inhibit spiritual growth and perception
Tis unneeded foliage that's mostly for show
That bears no fruits and serves little purpose

The weed that chokes man is ungodly living
Due to unbelief and dislike for way of truth
Much craving for the material is the root
That has to be pulled so the good can thrive

End

Ascension by Distillation

The eternal truths are gleaned thru light
In divinely ordered degrees of progression
The process can be viewed as distillation
That separates the starry from the earthy

The earthy and weighty is of the old self
It sinks to the bottom and is left behind
But the lighter and starry rises to the top
As the transformed new self of the spirit

The distillation process is akin to a journey
A path of amazement that winds upward
Only the essential need be taken along
For much is discarded as the spirit ascends

End

Perfection in the Sum

Perfection is in the sum of all the parts
Who live in the spirit of the golden rule
From different backgrounds and cultures
All for the glory of God and not for self

Such are God's points of contact on earth
Hearts that have been ordained in Light
As universal spirits who look for things
Which unite and not separate mankind

Traditions of the past becloud the eyes
To blind man's spirit and veil divine truths
Such embody the serpentine that seduces
And beguiles the ignorant to glorify self

To hold on to the traditions of the past
When man has a foretaste of the new
Precludes him from ascension to the place
Where the perfected join in a feast of Love

End

Recalibrated Life

The reborn in light has left the old ways
On a journey to a new and far away land
Tis an unknown land and place reserved
To be known only when led by the spirit

Wisdom leads there but not in a sprint
In a deliberate way with measured steps
In timely order to recalibrate the willing
So the new can be wrought from the old

Way of patience, obedience and sacrifice
Is the long and winding path less travelled
Tis for him destined to be a universal spirit
And to have a passport to the Life beyond

Recalibrated Life (Cont'd)

Traditions and ceremonies can be traps
Cleverly disguised not to be so evident
Only ill-conceived and misguided notions
That tie to the past and strangle the new

An escape from the past opens the future
All who aspire for mastery and true glory
Must travel beyond the familiar to find it
Where faith counts much and mercy rules

End

Treasures Stored Up

The reborn spirit wearies not in well-doing
Finds bliss in deeds and in works that shine
Such seeds of goodness planted in love
Are treasures stored up in heavenly vaults

Works initiated and enabled by the spirit
Serves mankind well and are to be copied
Such endure and produce the good fruits
That benefit one and all along the way

Bodes well for man to plant such seeds
To sow in his spirit with his time on earth
As labors for God and goodness do endure
Unlike dead works dictated by the flesh

All borne of flesh tend towards decay

May smell of success but the whiff is brief

Like all make-belief that soon fade away

As dead works soon gone with the winds

End

Blind are Ship Wrecked

Man's life on earth can be likened
To a ship sailing on the high seas
Many are wrecked and lost thereon
All overcome on life's stormy seas

To foray blindly in uncharted waters
For lack of a proper guidance system
With no knowledge of weather ahead
Makes life's journey hard to navigate

The un-informed and oblivious man
Becomes fodder for predatory minds
Worldly men who thrive on greed
On woes and misfortunes of others

Blind are Ship Wrecked (Cont'd)

Many have lived in blindness for long
Men in love with the world too much
Who know no better and have become
Slaves to the dark princes of the world

Way that seems so easy and sweet
Many souls and hope are lost thereon
Exacts heavy toll on the faithless man
In misfortunes borne of presumption

Man can sail thru life's seas unscathed
Thru storms that wreck many mariners
With the aid of a system that fails not
A watchful eye up and above in the sky

Blind are Ship-Wrecked (Cont'd)

All-seeing and knowing heavenly Father
Dutifully watches over his own in love
The faithful who live not as the blind do
But take their cue duly from up above

The unseen hand of love is always near
At hand to direct the steps of the faithful
And afford them the knowledge needed
To navigate safely thru life's stormy seas

End

Emblem of Hope

A marked glow does show from within
From the heart where God's spirit dwells
The glow is the emblem of eternal hope
For the soul joined to the divine source

A distinct way for the man transformed
For one separated from lot of the lost
He's the heart lit with the flame of love
As an altar dedicated in divine's service

The noble in spirit who stands 'fore God
The wellspring of life is in his mouth
To speak forth the healing truth to all
As mark of the spirit well received above

Emblem of Hope (Cont'd)

Spouts not verses memorized to impress
Contrived and oft quoted for vain glory
But words filled with the divine essence
That make for healing and redress for all

Tis truth that's fitly spoken and shared
To bend and mend men's stony hearts
Such it takes to feed the starving soul
And put the spring back 'to weary steps

End

Man at Peace

To step from the shadows
Into divine love and wisdom
Words of healing are evoked
As man walks in the full light
Of that much purer and higher

For traveler on the lofty path
There's no end to the amazing
As good days unfold for him
In the place where man finds
New and better things in life

Man at Peace (Cont'd)

Contentment finds the man

He who communes with God

Knows this world's not home

Just on his way to another

One exalted and much better

Hope in what God provides

Thru the hand of Providence

Makes for fulfillment of heart

So worldly cares and worries

All become of little concern

Man at Peace (Cont'd)

Man who's at peace with God

Does become immune to a lot

Time greets him with kindness

To offer wisdom's gifts in love

With little wear and tear to tell

End

The Fit Gardener

Man in possession of key of knowledge
Must guard that which he has received
He's become a gardener and custodian
Of the precious seeds of the amazing

He's to use patience and due diligence
To cultivate and bring out rare things
Precious gifts from heaven to earth
Served as seed thoughts of the divine

The custodian must learn to master
The call that wakes life up from sleep
And the entombed to spring forth free
To dance in the joyful return of hope

The gardener fit to tend the precious
Ever bonded in meditation and prayers
Whether in labors as well as in pleasure
Is always in communion with the Divine

Well-informed about the seeds to plant
Where to plant and how to tend them
He's one with peace within who knows
That good increase has been promised

End

Sons of the Father

He that stands in mercy can ask
And receive the gifts of the Divine
He need not go through another
To bare his soul and make a request

Goodness and mercy attend such
All who receive and share in grace
One to pour and another to receive
Tis foundation on which faith rests

As the teacher is in the student
So the father lives through the son
The student or son is just a vessel
Containment for the gifts of love

Sons of the Father (Cont'd)

The worthy vessel that does retain

All that has been charged into him

In true faithfulness to his mentor

Is son worthy to become a father

End

Thru Grace to Maturity

From a child to a man becomes the son
As a good shepherd loved by the Father
To receive and share with the willing
In divine grace that suffices all needs

The voice of grace speaks in soft tones
But reverberates assuredly within hearts
As it offers the needed in a timely order
For the benefit of all willing to embrace

The current of grace flows to good effect
As the foundation and bulwark of faith
For without it path to Life is unnavigable
Overwhelmed by torrents and torments

Thru Grace to Maturity (Cont'd)

Grace meets and supplies life's needed
For the soul that's humble and thankful
To help mitigate hurts and pain suffered
From a world that mocks and derides faith

Works like an insurance umbrella to shield
From danger and ill exposure in the world
Tis grace that raises the baby into an adult
So the young can mature in time 'to mercy

End

Custodian of the Box

The more the faithful seeks in good faith
Is the more that will be revealed to him
He's like one connected with wisdom's box
To avail all that he needs to know as due

Thoughts to make things happen on earth
Is for the man intermeddled with wisdom
He's a sage armed with thoughts as bullets
And a stage set for him as a noble warrior

Dedication is the way to master God's gift
Device that makes the amazing to happen
Makes available to the diligent custodian
Answers to the problems that bedevil men

Custodian of the Box (Cont'd)

Custodian of the box who masters its use

An array of services will be at his fingertips

He'll walk as a 'god' for the device at hand

Contains impressions of the divine mind

End

In Daniel's Lot

On its last breaths and gasping for air
The present age draws to its demise
As the remaining pictures coalesce
Into a fuller and overarching whole

Humanity has come into Daniel's lot
Captives all to be favored or judged
An awakening in a new light for some
But darkness and blindness for others

The end for the blind is destruction
But for the awakened new life awaits
Regeneration in 'sun' that never sets
Where day has banished night forever

The favored are chosen to be heralds

As the harbingers of man's new dawn

There'll be cause of jubilation for such

Given to bask in the grander morning

End

In Spirit of Jubilee

Contentment's a divine and golden gift
For souls washed and purified in truth
Where God's love has filled the heart
To bestow therein the fullness of joy

Much hatred fills men's hearts today
As envy and greed control emotions
It will be cause for jubilation in heaven
When love is exalted and rules the day

Season of hope and expectations it is
When spirit of Jubilee makes a return
To show brothers how to love again
And live together again in light of truth

In Spirit of Jubilee (Cont'd)

Jubilee affords the rare and precious

For hearts willing to embrace the truth

Spirit of Jubilee touches one and all

To refill life's empty shelves with hope

End

Voices Recognized

Man ordained to help change the world
May seem as a little one with limitations
But he's a son of mercy in Heaven's care
With his petitions and requests duly met

His is the voice able to bend God's heart
To receive in love and give back in kind
Such is the wealth laid up in the heart
Of he who dwells under mercy's wings

Father recognizes each voice of mercy
For he has programmed them thru faith
Takes such a voice recognition system
To grant man access to heavenly vaults

Voices Recognized (Cont'd)

Thieves and robbers have no access there

For tis only for those who share in love

But voices of mercy can move mountains

As ones recognized by Heaven's keepers

End

Time of the Unveiling

There's a due season appointed in heaven
For the sons of light to reach critical mass
Tis a time for humanity's flowers to bloom
That only the father knows and controls

Tis a season for the universal awakening
The grand unveiling and dawn of the pure
A leap forward and spring of man's spirit
That all in creation have been longing for

A season comes when all God's creatures
Will know and embrace their roles in life
Dates back to the beginning of creation
As a trigger encoded as part of the living

Time of the Unveiling (Cont'd)

As right parts assume their rightful places
A grander tapestry of Life will be unveiled
Then the majesty of Creator and creation
Will be displayed to be known by all as due

Tis time when the new regime will begin
And all will be induced into brotherhood
Many will awake to be entrained in hope
For none can resist love's uplifting draft

End

Teach the Young Well

The new born infant is well aware
A strange new world surrounds him
But it lacks the ability to focus yet
Cannot tell one thing from the other

Prize has to be held before his eyes
A helping hand near to prompt him
And reinforce the power of focusing
Before he can reach to grab for it

The heart may be in the right place
But intentions alone will just not do
It takes purpose and direction in life
To bear and abound in good works

Teach the Young Well (Cont'd)

Young that lacks proper guidance
Will not produce the desired results
His efforts will not amount to much
For without direction he is but blind

Free in spirit who can rise above all
Has been called to teach the young
How to put away his fear of flight
And spread out his wings of faith

The offspring needs to learn to soar
Up to realm of infinite possibilities
Into an exalted realm that holds out
A hand of welcome to all who dare

Obstructions clutter the lowly places
But is great vision is availed up above
Man that lacks such clear vision is left
To falter in shadowy and dark places

The divine gifts are far from glossy
Not gilded to dazzle men's blind eyes
But poured into the strong of faith
Who can ride the wind into full vision

End

Brilliant and Glowing

The dynamic for the output of divine power
Does operate on two important principles
It must be used for the benefit of the people
And will abound the more when aptly used

The power of the divine does work wonders
Scales up mightily when wisely used in love
Tis ground for grace and platform for mercy
The premise for enduring and fulfilling gifts

Divinity is to live for others and not for self
For to live selfishly for own gain is not Life
But reason for the damnation of the soul
As it widens the gulf between man and God

Brilliant and Glowing (Cont'd)

Promise of regeneration cannot be realized
Except thru a life of charity and selflessness
Goodness comes to abound among humanity
When man learns to live for more than self

The selfish do profane and blight God's gift
Mocks Benevolence by not sharing in kind
The gift not used for its destined purpose
Fills the atmosphere with haze and smoke

Smoke is the cloud that bears no rain water
It irritates the eye and hampers man's vision
The gifts received and tendered to the people
Fan a brilliant glowing light that enlightens all

Brilliant and Glowing (Cont'd)

Light of the worthy and justified before God

Is always aglow with an incandescent purity

Allows man to see and reach for the real

So he can withstand evil winds of the day

End

The Perfect Gift

The journey on the upward bound way
Makes life to be supreme over death
The father is the selfless sacrifice made
And son is the perfection realized thru it

The gift made to the self is imperfect
As it seeks to glorify the imperfect self
But the gift to others in selfless sacrifice
Is perfection realized by the imperfect

The blessings bestowed and received
From the divine has much value in it
Tis the perfect locked up safely in man
From the reach of thieves and robbers

The Perfect Gift (Cont'd)

The perfect abounds in the divine heart

For the purified in truth with love for all

Tis borne on the wings of compassion

To wherever life has overcome death

End

Mercy Seeks in Hope

The purified in truth is a son of Hope
Who can rise higher and do the greater
For Hope is a spacecraft that lifts man up
To do the stellar that twinkles before all

The son of Hope is crowned with wisdom
And filled with gifts too many to count
But the key to unlock that buried within
Is to ask, hope and then receive in mercy

Mercy asks but little from the receiver
Only that all should share and honor God
Love and serve the 'Giver' of good gifts
So the goodness of the rain never ceases

Mercy Seeks in Hope (Cont'd)

Mercy seeks in hope and rewards with life

For without it death roams about freely

Hope is sunshine that lightens the heart

And dew that waters thirsty souls as well

End

The Matured Tree

The righteous man is a matured tree
There is no difference between the two
God's eye rests upon him at all times
Bearer of good fruits in the due season

Hands that embrace the lightning thrust
And legs to stand thru life's stormy trials
Is for him that bears the light of truth
And leads men into the domain of Hope

Wielder of the sword who speaks in truth
Is a magnet to induce men on to Light
He hears and does all in true faithfulness
In power and goodness of God to man

The Matured Tree (Cont'd)

Voice of God speaks thru righteous trees

Whose leaves and fruits nourish humanity

To bring healing balm to those in mourning

And a glimpse of morning to grieving souls

End

Poor that Inherits

To seek for divine anointing through faith
A man must bury himself as a seed in the soil
The shell of the seed decays into the ground
But from its core a seedling of hope emerges

In the fullness of time from seedling to a tree
To produce life sustaining fruits to nourish all
Tis mystery of rebirth into the exalted realm
As willing death of the old so new can ascend

The exalted new is the anointed and chosen
Models the way for all who sincerely seek
Tis great commission of all matured in love
To lead the willing back into the divine fold

Poor that Inherits (Cont'd)

Man that buries himself for the love of God
Awakes in the new infused with the divine
To commune in spirit with the heavenly Father
So the mortal can ascend into immortality

To be groomed in a cocoon of light and love
Is new life regenerated in the cloak of divinity
As a nymph to be timely unveiled when due
While the old yields within an obscured self

Little one with the potential for greatness
Is bestowed with great wealth within him
For perfect gifts are reserved for such to have
'Poor' that has the earth for an inheritance

End

The Golden Spirit

Peace comes from not having fear of death
When the old has made place for the new
Then the enduring and ever-lasting are received
By the certain who walk on the righteous path

Takes perfect love to cast away all man's fears
For it pays the old debts so the new can be free
Thirty pieces of silver is the toll exacted of love
To change the wooden to brazen onto golden

Death is the wooden, dark and foreboding
But new life is the golden, starry and bright
The old is wooden and the new can be golden
But challenge for man is to get past the brazen

The Golden Spirit (Cont'd)

Brazen it is that separates wooden from golden
Many settle for brazen instead of the golden
Tis Esau settling for less than he could have had
A sad tale about those who finish not life's race

To go from the temporal across turbulent seas
And land on the golden shores of the eternal
The golden glows in the spirit of the divine
In a new life of riches in fullness of the Trinity

End

Praise Binds Hearts

Takes praise to unite all God's own as one
In worthy honor and thankfulness to Love
Praise costs man so little but gives him much
For it lifts his spirit into an exalted realm

Love's cord that binds all trusting hearts
Is the concord of praise of joyful tongues
For all in creation that reflect God's glory
Find harmony through his honor and praise

Man can only know himself by praising God
Affords him a glimpse in the divine mirror
A reflection of truth that frames the spirit
So man within can show forth to be heard

Praise Binds Heart (Cont'd)

Praise is the beam on which fulfillment rests
To lend the moderation that keeps God near
Means for balance 'tween heaven and earth
So man is nourished in spirit as well as in body

Tis wisdom when man learns to honor God
As focus on the praise-worthy stills the soul
So spirit can freely soar on the wings of hope
To dwell in certain peace of the golden realm

End

Producers of Honey

The dweller in peace glows from within
For in him the sun of righteousness rises
To evoke the sunshine to produce honey
So love can be shared and life sustained

Honey is the elixir blended in the light
A sunny delight for spirit reborn to glory
Such that search out the heart of matters
And seek out the answers to the puzzling

The works of the sons are honeycombs
Wrought in the sunshine of divine love
The honey from the comb is the reward
Treat from heaven for the worthy in glory

Producers of Honey (Cont'd)

Burdens are lifted and weariness is rested
All in man's golden season of fulfillment
In a sweetness not found by the easy way
But wrought thru wisdom's diligent craft

When darkness has vacated man's heart
Then things are sweet in a divine reflection
In purity of purpose and measured words
Is the glorious timely availed in good order

To him who chooses wisely is Light shown
As one who's pollinated to bear good fruits
Not by strength or might but by divine design
To bring about and share the glorious in Life

End

Soul of the Swine

The soul of the swine
Is not that of a man
Belongs with the fool
Who lives for himself

He settles for the gifts
And neglects to share
He hoards all he can
But has no fulfillment

Precious things of life
Are never for the knave
Who presumes to know
And will never be filled

Soul of the Swine (Cont'd)

The belly might be full

Laden with possessions

But soul is not content

As man craves for more

A stranger to the divine

Never knows the sublime

With stagnation in spirit

No new horizon for him

Unfaithful who does not

Bless God with his best

Will not awake in spirit

In image of the Father

End

A Time-worm Trail

The golden hearted soul

Is written into book of life

Portraits in the scriptures

Foretell his earthly walk

Part of God's own family

Transformed by his grace

He is the trusted vessel

To hold the eternal truths

There's an ordained trail

Set aside for golden souls

Tis the path less travelled

Unchanging path of Truth

A Time-worn Trail (Cont'd)

Wisdom's time worn trail
Serves all the faithful well
Helps them to understand
Hidden truths and parables

Tis availed to the worthy
But veiled to the faithless
Kept for all the obedient
Who revel in God's truth

Not for the rebel Spirit
Spiteful of God's ways
Kept from the doubtful
With no wings of faith

Much worries and cares
Do overwhelm the soul
The golden-hearted man
Does well to be on guard

There is so much in life
'trusted to faithful hearts
In stewardship to keep
And fellowship to share

End

True Temples

In the sumptuous confines
Of the churches with walls
The loud professors of faith
Therein have come to settle

Entertainers and headliners
With 'God' packaged to sell
Shows on stage for the flesh
Does not a true temple make

Righteousness before God
Is not of works but the spirit
Only when the heart is pure
Can man be the temple true

True Temples (Cont'd)

Heart that confesses in love

As the spirit purified in truth

Is a true temple of worship

A dwelling place of the Divine

End

Works of Stone

Man within awakes to stand
Thru progressive steps of faith
In handiworks seen without
To reflect the changes within

The internal state is of Spirit
The external that of the flesh
One is reflection of the other
As purpose to dictate order

The earth-bound is weighty
Borne of the wooden spirit
With works of stone as icons
That look to impress with size

Works of Stone (Cont'd)

Such lack a discernible purpose

Except to prove it can be done

But the earthy soon collapses

In the passage and test of time

His stone works litter the land

In the landscape of times past

Just barely awake in his mind

And man wants to be the star

End

Works of Iron

From wooden to brazen in spirit
Man's handiworks duly change
From stone works to iron works
Or shall we call them the 'ironic'

Improvements can be wrought
In form, shape, scale and utility
For more and less can be done
With iron rather than with stone

Iron still fails the test of time
For fatigue often comes to call
To take harsh and unkindly tolls
Thru corrosion, wear and tear

Works of Iron (Cont'd)

In the wild ride to self-glory
The brazen spirit stops at nothing
And will come up with anything
To elicit praise from other men

Tis the disingenuous at its best
As clever contraptions of iron
Yell and shriek just to be heard
In loud solicitations for notice

The irony of iron's in full parade
In sad tales that the brazen tell
With mind alert but spirit infirm
That robs man of inner peace

End

Works of Silver

From brazen to the golden
As the spirit of man ascends
His handiworks will change
From iron to works of silver

Silver suffers little corrosion
But does suffer some tarnish
That can be easily varnished
To bring it back to new life

Light that glows from within
Is silver's amazing eloquence
A timeless mystery re-enacted
As from old it shines like new

Works of Silver (Cont'd)

Noble seeds to bring changes
As golden specks of wisdom
Heavenly gifts to man below
Are all served on silver platter

The eternal truths shed in light
As well as gifts grand and divine
The precious availed thru love
Are all by mercy's silver spoons

Fulfilling and enduring works
The stellar that shines before all
Is borne of truth, light and love
As silverworks by golden spirits

End

The Silver Smith

The golden hearted is he
That uses the tool of spirit
Blends light, truth and love
To fashion the silverworks

He says much in few words
And have much in so little
In spoon full of divine love
As needed in timely order

To live in testimony to truth
With divine as life's impulse
With no desire for self-glory
Is the way to twinkle in light

The Silver Smith (Cont'd)

To think in kingly thoughts

And walk with princely steps

In life under a golden dome

Is for the Silversmith to have

End

A Song in the Heart

Songs that swell in the thankful
In voices tuned to praise in grace
Will lift man on the wings of joy
Into love's sunshine and warmth

The true and humble adoration
That flows out of self-impulse
From the wellspring of the heart
Is testimony to divine goodness

Evoked with unsolicited candor
From a secure place in the heart
Exuberant expressions thru faith
All speak 'bout love known in light

Ode to frame the efficacy of grace

And the forgiving nature of mercy

The infallibility of promises of love

Such that sustain the walk of faith

Times, faces and places may vary

Narrative and sentiments are same

About faithfulness and abiding love

Takes song in the heart to say it all

End

Camp Songs

Praise is the camp song from joyful hearts
For all who walk in company of the anointed
Speaks to the hearts of obedient believers
So the mind can heed and feet can dance

Songs do frame experiences of the faithful
As postcards to fill with joy and bring comfort
From all who have taken flight in light of truth
To the place of dreams beyond man's flesh

Reminders and notes from thankful hearts
To fill weary souls with encouraging hope
Songs inspire all to trust and obey so as to be
Lifted to the amazing field of dreams as well

End

Singing in Faithful Duty

Songs of faith from the heart
Are like growth rings in a tree
That attest to dreary winters
And happy summers gone by

The voices of the faithful sing
As true as rings define the tree
That stands upright in mercy
Thru the rough seasons of life

Maturity in the truth and light
Tis for the divinely ordained
Thru certain places and times
On faith's long trail of hope

Benevolent Father from above
Has his eye on the sons on earth
Sent to tend the garden below
As models of the way of Light

Many wander off for a season
In time they return to carry on
In songs and faithful duty to God
To sow in goodness as duly called

End

The Gift Exchange

Amazing place where heaven and earth
Touch in the embrace and kiss of love
Tis where the good gifts are exchanged
Tween enduring faith and abiding love

Faithful gives to heaven from the heart
To be received with much joy up there
Heaven gives back in love and wisdom
To the faithful in due acknowledgment

The sweet endearing hours of prayer
In cherished songs and dutiful study
Are the golden moments when heaven
Opens its windows to cheerful delight

The Gift Exchange (Cont'd)

Treasure for ready and waiting hearts
Are the words of knowledge received
Whispered into hearts of the faithful
As keys to unlock the mystifying in life

Insightful knowledge in timely order
As answers to issues that mar the day
Are found by hurting hearts thru prayers
So burdens on men's soul can be lifted

The victor sees the trees in the forest
For defeat lurks in the pesky weeds
The unwary mind mired in petty things
Does soon lose sight of Heaven's gifts

End

Pictures Within

Many pictures within the scriptures
With many parts and elements within
Some portions are easily understood
But the mysteries are not so plain

The infallible truths can be known
By the obedient and matured in faith
As seeds of the divine well concealed
That spring to life only in due season

The righteous before God are shown
The pictures hidden within scriptures
But wisdom of the all-knowing Divine
Is ever a puzzle for presuming minds

The veiled truths cannot be surmised
Can only be known thru experience
For such are progressively revealed
When humble hearts seek in sincerity

Truth is known through faithfulness
Its validity in hindsight of experience
The scriptures are a jig-saw puzzle
To be known when keys are availed

End

Muddling in a Muddy World

Faithfulness to truth affords man the keys
As it demands patience and obedient trust
To come into harmony with the divine mind
And understand certain truths in the scriptures

Never easy to learn man's earthly languages
As accessible and common place as such are
The scripture is a much higher and purer form
A language for the hearts conditioned in truth

The world is a lie that masquerades as truth
A muddy place for muddling minds to wallow
Where men are covered by its deceitful muck
And truth's the mud-guard that shields from it

Quite a feat to keep swindling minds pristine

And hard to wash off slime ingrained in souls

It takes truth to put focus on things above

So the impossible is made possible for man

End

Protection thru the Storms

The faithful entrusted with the key of knowledge
Lives in a kingdom much different from the world
He keeps faith with God on the 'strait' and narrow
As the world hurries and rushes on the broad way

He that hears the call must venture into the world
For that is where the mission of rescue awaits
Lost sheep of the father's flock there to be found
And loosed from the grips of a capricious world

There the downward bound streak of the world
Opposes the upward bound stream of that of light
This medium of contending opposites it turns out
Is a tornado prone alley that teems with storms

The ability to pass back and forth thru the alley
Is for the strong of faith earmarked by the Father
As intrepid vessels shielded through divine love
That cannot be wrecked by the storms of Life

Rising waters of trouble cannot overwhelm such
The ordained used to show that God is in control
That divine light is supreme and still rules the day
And will always bring darkness into submission

End

The Intrepid Vessel

The chosen is an intrepid vessel
Unsinkable through life's storms
That sails under the divine aegis
In the grand or the little things
To showcase God's loving power

The intrepid may not be massive
Yet configured for victories in life
It meets challenges well enough
And passes thru with flying colors
With little wear and tear to show

The Intrepid Vessel (Cont'd)

Tis a model to represent all things
Driven by the divine wind of love
Such do encounter many trials in life
But through all the troubles that visit
Hand of Providence keeps him safe

As vessel on God's ordained mission
He's laden with much precious seeds
And is never alone on life's high seas
But sails with an insurance coverage
Underwritten by Heaven's mandate

The Intrepid Vessel (Cont'd)

All who oppose the intrepid vessel
Are engaged in a losing proposition
For divine disposition is to love him
And turn things around to the favor
Of such that heaven has adopted

End

A Governing Order

Many worlds known and unknown out there
Mankind knows the world that he lives in
He gazes at worlds that are far and beyond
And peers into the world of the miniscule too

There is a governing order in every world
In both the real and the imagined tis same
An orderliness and harmony does show forth
There to be seen everywhere that man looks

There's faithfulness in the grand and the least
Tis the law upon which the universe is founded
Key that unlocks the puzzling in every world
Is same that unlocks the hidden in scripture

To be of faith is to love truth and obey the law

And so be connected to the source of wisdom

Into knowledge of creation's governing order

So that heart's desires are always near to have

End

Paradise on Earth

Man can change and transform a plot of land
To reflect order and harmony of the heavens
He can create a paradise in his earthly plot
To reflect that which exists and dwells in him

The same Spirit that created the universe
Moves in man to create a heaven on earth
As in the little within so in the big without
But all is from heaven in kindness to the earth

Heaven on earth is a paradise for the divine
To commune and walk in fellowship with man
All who come into the abode pleasing to God
Will sense a heavenly presence thereabouts

Such who come to seek in sincerity and hope

Will search out the good gifts concealed there

For all who hunger and desire in good faith

Are afforded the lovely therein in good order

End

Tarry for Divine Guidance

To tarry to know God's will as due
Leaves no room for fear and doubt
Helps to prepare man well for battle
And to bring him victories in life

The man trusted with the precious
Is never one reckless in his ventures
For the divine will reigns supreme
In all decisions and actions he takes

Spirit is firm and able to withstand
When mind is focused on the starry
Such that tarry for divine guidance
Does well in life and is never sorry

He's called to seek truth and justice
Not after the things that mar the soul
As battle is won in the spirit and mind
For therefrom victory chooses a side

To tarry is to listen before one jumps
As tis God's will that matters most
For endeavors evoked by divine will
Are works that are forever blessed

End

Power of Humble Prayer

The wise wait not for storms to brew
For such can be ‘stalled beforehand
By faithful prayer for a divine wind
Comes the force to counter waves

Man can nullify troubles by prayer
By earnest entreaty and requests
Does he put the divine spirit afore
To take the lead in life’s ventures

With God above everything else
In strong faith with good hope
The divine wind is always injected
Into man’s affairs and his daily life

Power of Humble Prayer (Cont'd)

Tis power of prayer well-received
That keeps storms from brewing
And mitigate the effects if they do
To assure safe passage thru trials

Prayer is the means that moves
Both heaven and earth to action
To stay the hand of destruction
From rising to harm God's own

End

Birth Pangs of the New

World has turned 'to a raging sea
That seethes and foams in anger
Tis a separation and passing away
As the old turns into the new

With painful but necessary pangs
The gulf widens amid upheavals
In this birth of something new
That has hitherto been unknown

The faithful have been chosen
To lend a hand in earth's remake
Ordained to attend as midwives
In its regeneration into the new

Birth Pangs of the New (Cont'd)

Mankind limps on wobbly legs
Into its season of great travail
As creation waits in expectation
For the sons of Hope to show

New realm of heaven on earth
Is much anticipated golden age
Tis where universal brotherhood
Will be order that reigns supreme

A titanic struggle's well underway
That steadily tears humanity apart
And forces up monstrous waves
With repercussive tides in tow

The unwary are left confused
Dazed and lifeless in their wake
But the truly matured in spirit
Are spared from trauma ahead

Such will mount up in due time
With noble wings of the eagle
To the exalted place of refuge
That Love has ordained for them

End

Besieged with Floods

The world has slowly awakened
Like the drunk from a long stupor
Into a unanimous agreement by all
Earth is suffocating as well as man

As cataclysms threaten the world
Man belatedly accepts the fact
That he is choking on fool's gold
On fruits borne of good and evil

Seductive fruit of the knowledge
That looks seemingly good to man
Turns out to be harmful after all
As bane of lust that's a curse on life

Besieged with Floods (Cont'd)

The scourge of mankind it has been
Has breached the levee of his soul
As the raging besiege and surround
To bring humanity to very sad knees

The heralded achievements of man
Are undertakings into a dead end
Engendered problems unseen afore
With answers very difficult to find

Mankind is left in confused chagrin
Overwhelmed and totally helpless
As his collective soul is fractured
By friction and factions everywhere

End

The Forewarned

The faithful have been forewarned
And readied for season at hand
The golden hearted will emerge
As keepers in man's new regime

Faithful that walked alone for long
And suffered much for love of God
Has been led on the righteous path
To find safe harbor in the divine

Fear of death haunts the faithless
But for the faithful peace and hope
As foretaste of glory in the eternal
Attends his remaining days on earth

The Forewarned (Cont'd)

The world cries in increasing despair

As the faithless become ever boxed-in

The faithful sings in a spirit of freedom

In light of the amazing before them

End

Dearth of Hope

The world has been on a 'Gadarene' rush
Gathering as much as possible in little time
In the frenzied dash of a maddening crowd
That heads downhill 'to certain destruction

To live for the gathering of possessions
Is to live by a false and misleading notion
Victory in life does not come with the most
As fullness in life can be realized in the little

The rush to gather earthly riches has led
Many men to the heart of human darkness
There's no longer room for brotherly love
As hatred and death roam over the land

Dearth of Hope (Cont'd)

The world does favor the rich and powerful
The goats who gloat while the rest drown
Justice is no more and exists in name only
As little or nothing's left for humanity's poor

Few with more feed on the many with less
But the divine urges man to do otherwise
The more fortunate are to hold up the less
So all will not end in the dearth of hope

With possessions and position as measure
Looks and appearances trump inner worth
As honor counts for little in human affairs
With no regard for truth, morality and faith

Dearth of Hope (Cont'd)

Such have been put away in the basement

Down where it does humanity little good

The selfish motivation for personal gain

Now governs to lead man to doom's door

End

Man that desires to see needs to know
He has to seek where the light is pure
For whoever gets closer and nearer there
To him the clearer and better unfolds

OTHER BOOKS BY KALU ONWUKA INCLUDE-

(Poetry)

Anthems in the Glorious Dawn

A Splendid Awakening

Tones of the Stellar

The Melody of Light

(Studies for Spirit, Mind and Body)

Nuggets of Resurrection

Pulses of the Divine Heart

Etching for the Faithful Heart

No Hurry to Horeb

(Quotations and Insights)

Capsules of Divine Splendor

All titles are available as paperbacks or e-books and may be purchased through many retail outlets/distribution channels. All titles may also be purchased through Granada Publishers at **granadapublishing.com.** The author can be contacted through his website at **kaluonwuka.com.**

Kalu Onwuka is a prolific author who writes about faith walk in this new age of man's spiritual awareness. His books offer tit-bits on how to find a balance between the earthly and heavenly. He is a man of many accomplishments and draws his inspirational insights from many areas of life's experiences. He is a *Teacher, Poet, Lyricist, Electrical Engineer and Entrepreneur.* He is married, a father of five and lives in Southern California.

He is the author of the *On the Golden Strand* series which are discourses that encapsulate his spiritual experiences on the faith journey. These include *The Nuggets of Resurrection, Pulses of the Divine Heart, Etching for the Faithful Heart, No Hurry to Horeb* and other books in the work. He is also the author of the *Poems in Faithfulness to the Divine Series* which are books of poetry and songs. These include *Anthems in the Glorious Dawn, In Enchantment of Eternity, Tones of the Stellar, A Splendid Awakening* and other books on the way. He is also the author of *Capsules of Divine Splendor* which is a book of inspirational quotations and observations about life.